A LOOK AT SPACE SCIENCE



# THE MOON

BY BERT WILBERFORCE

Gareth Stevens Publishing

CRASHCOURSE

**Please visit our website, www.garethstevens.com. For a free color catalog of all our high-quality books, call toll free 1-800-542-2595 or fax 1-877-542-2596.**

**Library of Congress Cataloging-in-Publication Data**
Names: Wilberforce, Bert, author.
Title: The moon / Bert Wilberforce.
Description: New York : Gareth Stevens Publishing, [2021] | Series: A look at space science | Includes bibliographical references and index. | Contents: Our amazing moon -- The moon's size -- What it's made of -- Moon craters -- Gravity and tides -- The moon's phases -- The lunar eclipse --The solar eclipse -- Exploring the moon -- Our moon's beginnings -- Our solar system's many moons.
Identifiers: LCCN 2019047293 | ISBN 9781538259283 (library binding) | ISBN 9781538259269 (paperback) | ISBN 9781538259276 | ISBN 9781538259290 (ebook)
Subjects: LCSH: Moon--Juvenile literature.
Classification: LCC QB582 .W55 2021 | DDC 523.3--dc23
LC record available at https://lccn.loc.gov/2019047293

First Edition

Published in 2021 by
**Gareth Stevens Publishing**
111 East 14th Street, Suite 349
New York, NY 10003



Designer: Sarah Liddell
Editor: Therese Shea

Photo credits: Cover, p. 1 (main) Vadim Sadovski/Shutterstock.com; background used throughout Zakharchuk/Shutterstock.com; p. 5 Siberian Art/Shutterstock.com; pp. 7, 17 Dima Zel/Shutterstock.com; p. 9 Procy/Shutterstock.com; p. 11 GHRevera/Wikimedia Commons; p. 13 Elena11/Shutterstock.com; p. 15 BlueRingMedia/Shutterstock.com; p. 19 Dennis van de Water/Shutterstock.com; p. 21 Natee Jitthammachai/Shutterstock.com; p. 23 (lunar eclipse) Changsgallery/Shutterstock.com; pp. 23 (diagram), 25 (diagram) In-Finity/Shutterstock.com; p. 25 (solar eclipse) THANAKRIT SANTIKUNAPORN/Shutterstock.com; p. 27 Xinhua News Agency/ Contributor/Xinhua News Agency/Getty Images; p. 29 CommonsHelper2 Bot/ Wikimedia Commons.



Printed in the United States of America



CPSIA compliance information: Batch #CS20GS: For further information contact Gareth Stevens, New York, New York at 1-800-542-2595.

# CONTENTS

Our Amazing Moon 4
The Moon's Size 6
What It's Made Of 10
Moon Craters 12
Gravity and Tides 14
The Moon's Phases 16
The Lunar Eclipse 22
The Solar Eclipse 24
Exploring the Moon 26
Our Moon's Beginnings 28
Our Solar System's Many Moons 30
Glossary 31
For More Information 32
Index 32

Words in the glossary appear in **bold** type the first time they are used in the text.

# OUR AMAZING MOON

The moon isn't just a pretty object in the night sky. It's a satellite of Earth. That means the moon orbits, or goes around, Earth. Life on Earth wouldn't be the same without it! Read on to learn more about our moon.

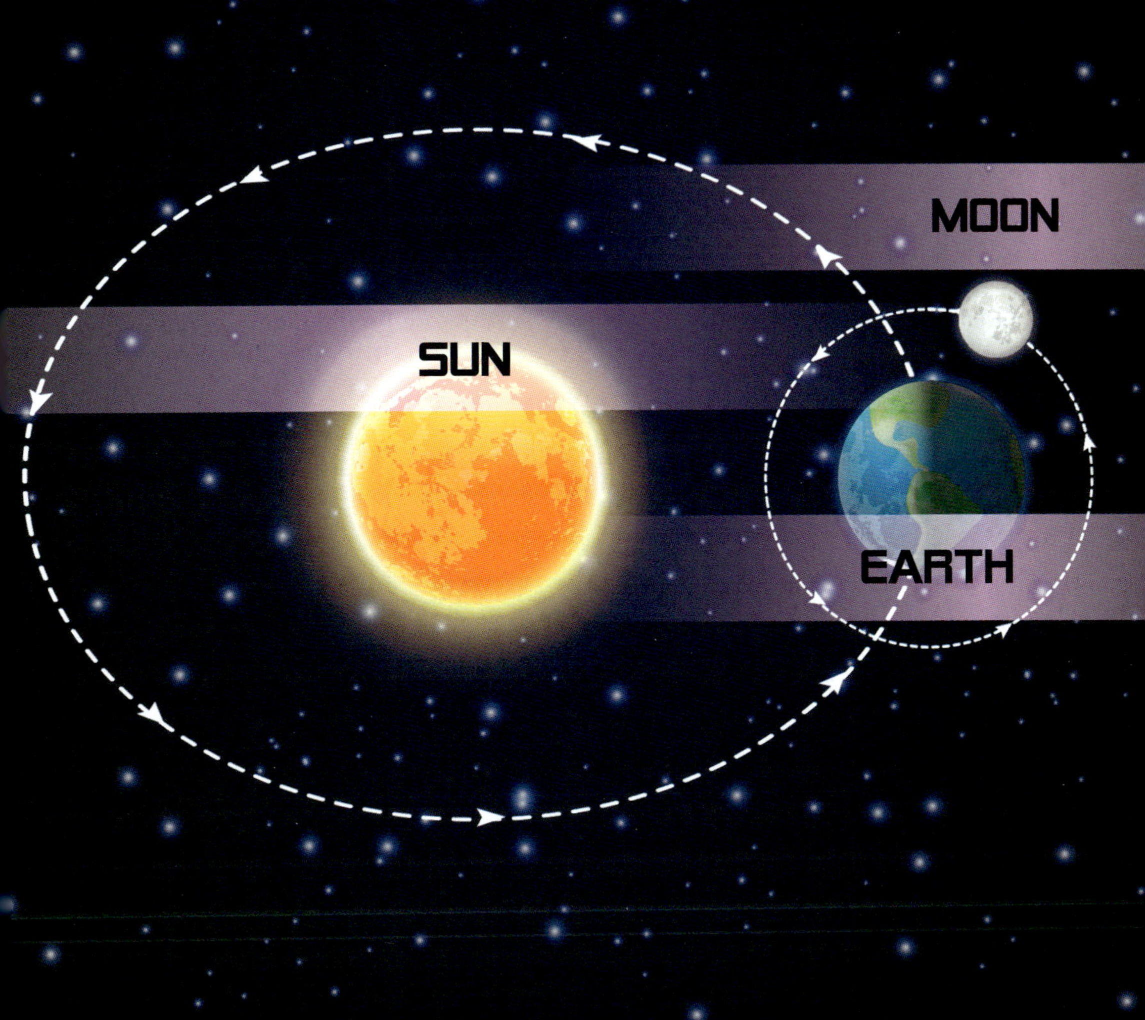


## MAKE THE GRADE

Earth is a satellite of the sun. Man-made machines that orbit Earth are also called satellites.

# THE MOON'S SIZE

The moon looks small to us, but it's not. In fact, it's one of the largest moons in the **solar system**. It's about 2,159 miles (3,475 km) across its middle. It measures about 6,784 miles (10,918 km) around.

## MAKE THE GRADE

The measurement across the center of a round object is called its diameter. The measurement around a round object is called its circumference.

The moon doesn't look big to us because it's about 238,855 miles (384,400 km) away. It doesn't travel in an exact circle around Earth, though. Sometimes it's closer, and sometimes it's farther away. It takes about 27 days to orbit Earth once.

PERIGEE

## MAKE THE GRADE

The moon's farthest point from Earth during its orbit is called the apogee. Its closest point is called the perigee.

# WHAT IT'S MADE OF

The moon is mostly made of rock. Its dusty, rocky **surface** is called regolith. The moon's dark areas are called maria. They once were filled with lava, or hot, liquid rock, from **volcanoes**! The moon's lighter areas are called highlands.

## MAKE THE GRADE

Scientists think the moon has a core, or center, made of **metal**.

# MOON CRATERS

The moon has thousands of pits on its surface. These are craters. They were made when bits of rock and metal from space hit the moon's surface. Some of these craters are **billions** of years old!

## MAKE THE GRADE

The moon has almost no **atmosphere.** That means no weather changes its surface like wind, rain, and other kinds of weather change Earth's surface.

# GRAVITY AND TIDES

The moon's **gravity** pulls on Earth. This causes the water on Earth closest to the moon to **swell**. This is called a high tide. The water farthest from the moon has a high tide too—because Earth is being pulled away from it!

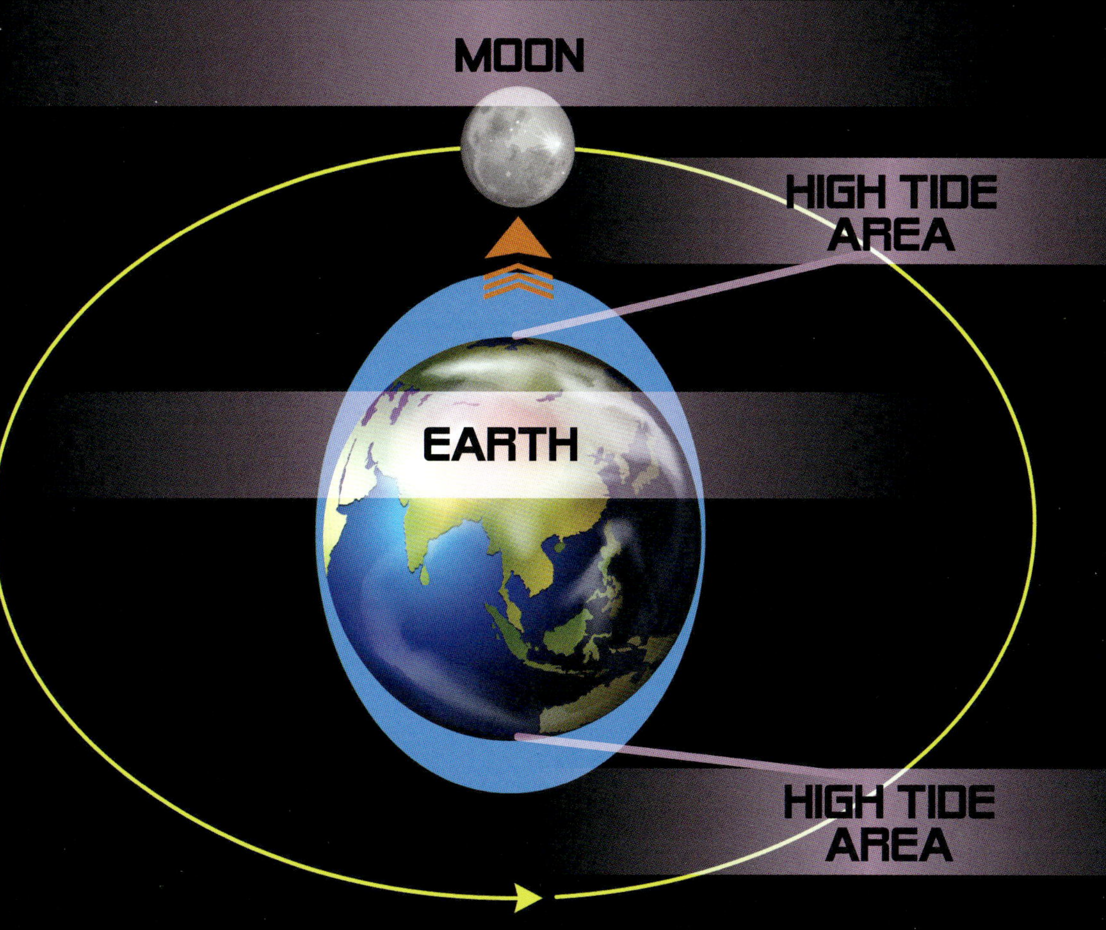


## MAKE THE GRADE

The amount of time between two high tides is around 12 hours and 25 minutes.

# THE MOON'S PHASES

You might wonder why the moon changes its shape every night. It doesn't! It just looks like that to us. The moon gives off no light of its own. Moonlight is sunlight reflecting, or bouncing off, the moon's surface.

## MAKE THE GRADE

The different shapes of the moon that we see are called phases. Certain phases of the moon have special names.

We see a new moon when the moon is between the sun and Earth. The moon looks dark because the sun is lighting the side we can't see. Each night after that, it waxes. That means the part we see gets larger.

## MAKE THE GRADE

A cycle is an order of events that repeats. One cycle of the moon's phases takes 29½ days.

When Earth is between the moon and the sun, we see a full moon. During this phase, the moon looks like a circle. After this, the moon wanes. That means it begins to look smaller each night until it's a new moon again.

## MAKE THE GRADE

A moon that looks more than half lit, but not full, is a gibbous moon. A moon that looks less than half lit is a crescent moon.

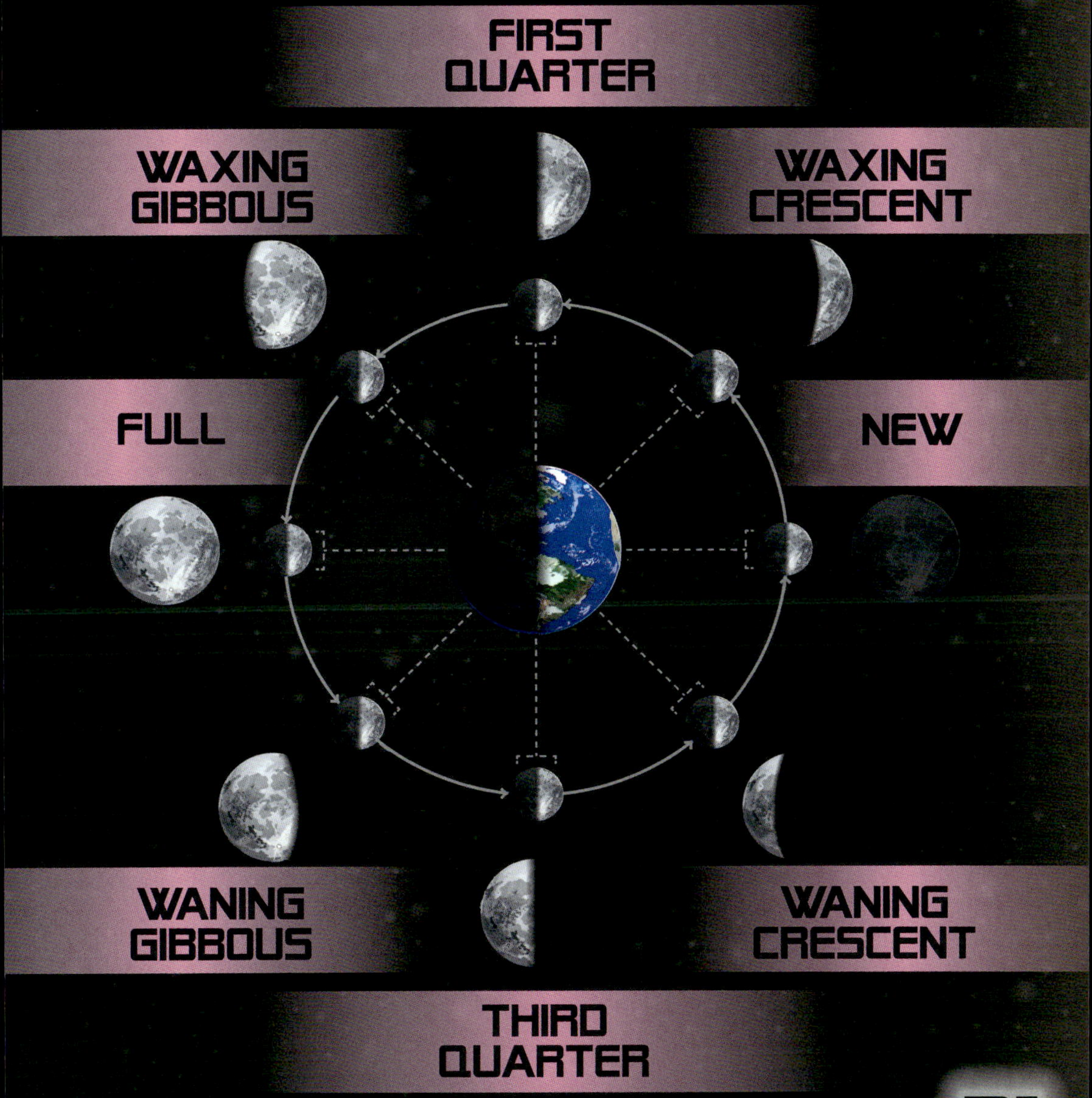

FIRST QUARTER

WAXING GIBBOUS

WAXING CRESCENT

FULL

NEW

WANING GIBBOUS

WANING CRESCENT

THIRD QUARTER

# THE LUNAR ECLIPSE

Sometimes during their movements, the moon, Earth, and the sun line up just right. Earth's shadow falls on the moon, blocking sunlight. Earth's atmosphere makes the moon look red or orange. This is called a total **lunar** eclipse.

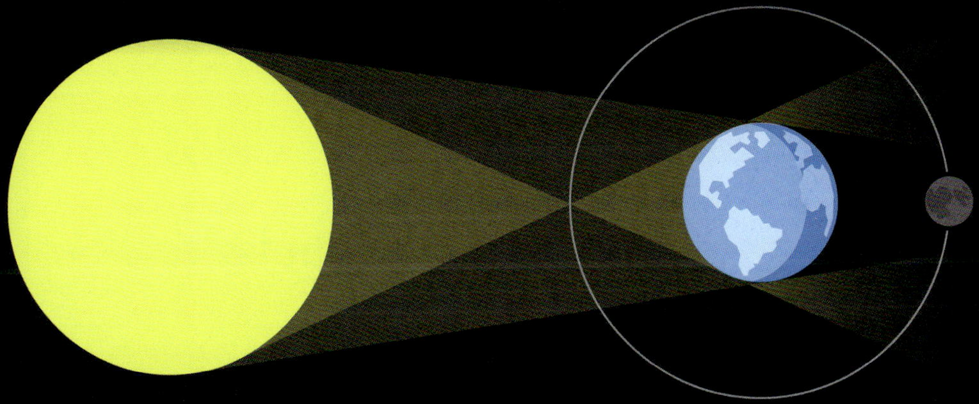

## MAKE THE GRADE

If Earth blocks just part of the sun's light from reaching the moon, we see a partial lunar eclipse.

# THE SOLAR ECLIPSE

Sometimes, as the moon orbits Earth, it blocks the sun. The moon looks like a black circle with a ring of light around it. This is called a total solar eclipse. "Solar" means having to do with the sun.

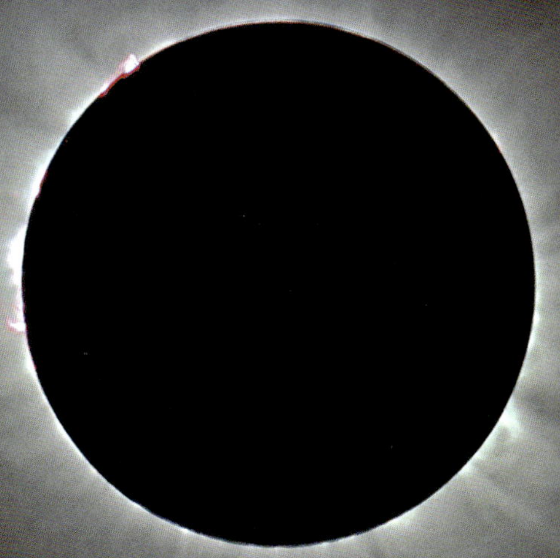

TOTAL SOLAR ECLIPSE

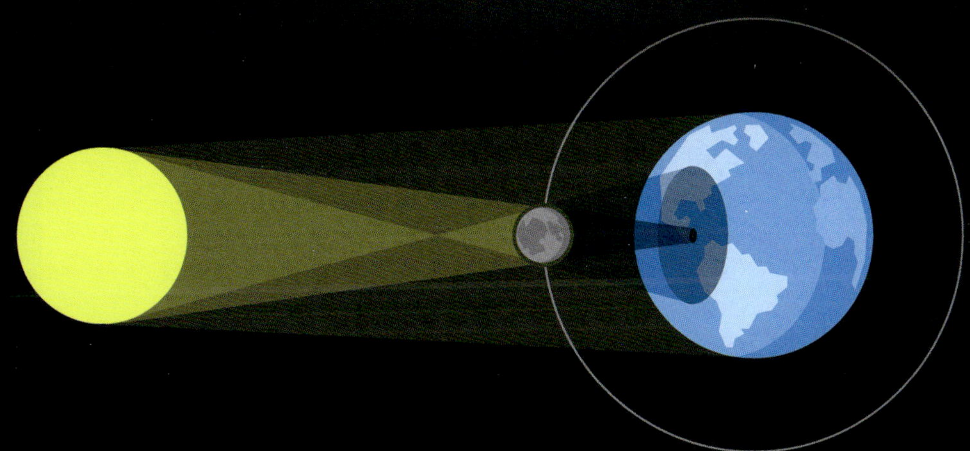

## MAKE THE GRADE

If the moon partly blocks the sun, it's called a partial solar eclipse. People can only watch solar eclipses with special glasses or other gear.

# EXPLORING THE MOON

On July 20, 1969, people finally landed on the moon! Neil Armstrong and Buzz Aldrin became the first humans to walk on the moon's surface. They brought back rocks for scientists to study. Other lunar **missions** took more **spacecraft** to the moon.

## MAKE THE GRADE

In 2019, China landed the first spacecraft on the moon's far side. We never see this side because the moon orbits Earth at about the same speed as it spins around.

# OUR MOON'S BEGINNINGS

Many scientists think the moon formed when an object about the size of Mars crashed into Earth. Gravity pulled pieces from the crash together and formed the moon. Learning about the moon helps us learn about the beginnings of our solar system!

## MAKE THE GRADE

Other **planets** and **dwarf planets** have moons. Scientists confirmed, or proved, asteroids can have moons too!

# OUR SOLAR SYSTEM'S MANY MOONS

| PLANET | CONFIRMED MOONS | UNCONFIRMED MOONS | TOTAL |
|---|---|---|---|
| Mercury | 0 | 0 | 0 |
| Venus | 0 | 0 | 0 |
| Earth | 1 | 0 | 1 |
| Mars | 2 | 0 | 2 |
| Jupiter | 53 | 26 | 79 |
| Saturn | 53 | 29 | 82 |
| Uranus | 27 | 0 | 27 |
| Neptune | 14 | 0 | 14 |
| **DWARF PLANETS** | | | |
| Pluto | 5 | 0 | 5 |
| Eris | 1 | 0 | 1 |
| Haumea | 2 | 0 | 2 |
| Makemake | 0 | 1 | 1 |
| Ceres | 0 | 0 | 0 |

# GLOSSARY

**atmosphere:** the mixture of gases that surround a planet

**billion:** 1,000 million, or 1,000,000,000

**dwarf planet:** a body, other than a moon, that orbits a star, has enough gravity to form a round shape, but hasn't cleared its orbit of small objects

**gravity:** the force that pulls objects toward the center of a planet, star, or moon

**lunar:** having to do with the moon

**metal:** a hard, shiny element found in the ground, such as iron or copper

**mission:** a task or job a group must perform

**planet:** a large round object that travels around a star that has cleared its orbit around the star

**solar system:** the sun and all the space objects that orbit it, including the planets and their moons

**spacecraft:** a vehicle used for traveling into space

**surface:** the top layer of a planet or moon

**swell:** to form a bulge, or look more full than normal

**volcano:** an opening in a planet's surface through which hot, liquid rock sometimes flows

# FOR MORE INFORMATION

## BOOKS

Buckley, James, Jr. *The Moon*. New York, NY: Penguin Young Readers, 2016.

Sommer, Nathan. *The Moon*. Minneapolis, MN: Bellwether Media, 2019.

## WEBSITES

**Facts About the Moon**
*www.natgeokids.com/au/discover/science/space/facts-about-the-moon*
How many of these lunar facts do you know?

**Moon**
*spaceplace.nasa.gov/search/moon/*
Check out this info provided by NASA.



# INDEX

Aldrin, Buzz 26
Armstrong, Neil 26
circumference 7
core 11
craters 12
cycle 19
diameter 7
Earth 4, 5, 8, 9, 13, 14, 18, 20, 22, 23, 24, 27, 28
gravity 14, 28
lunar eclipse 22, 23
phases 17, 19, 20
rocks 10, 12, 26
solar eclipse 24, 25
sun 5, 18, 20, 22, 23, 24, 25
tides 14, 15